*Quick*GUIDES
everything you need to know...fast

Staff Recruitment

by Caroline Hukins

reviewed by Judy Hare

WIREMILL
PUBLISHING LTD

Across the world the organizations and institutions that fundraise to finance their work are referred to in many different ways. They are charities, non-profits or not-for-profit organizations, non-governmental organizations (NGOs), voluntary organizations, academic institutions, agencies, etc. For ease of reading, we have used the term Nonprofit Organization, Organization or NPO as an umbrella term throughout the *Quick*Guide series. We have also used the spellings and punctuation used by the author.

Published by
Wiremill Publishing Ltd.
Edenbridge, Kent TN8 5PS, UK
info@wiremillpublishing.com
www.wiremillpublishing.com
www.quickguidesonline.com

British Library Cataloguing in Publication Data
A catalogue record for this book is available from the British Library.

ISBN Number 1-905053-02-9

Printed by Rhythm Consolidated Berhad, Malaysia
Cover Design by Jennie de Lima and Edward Way
Design by Colin Woodman Design

CONTENTS

STAFF RECRUITMENT

This guide provides help and advice on managing the entire recruitment process – from reviewing a vacancy to advertising and preparing recruitment literature to short-listing and interviewing and to hiring the successful candidate.

Hiring a staff member can be done in an hour, but the repercussions stay with an organisation for many years. It is worth taking time to think about the needs of the post and the process of recruitment, to ensure that the final decision maximises the opportunity afforded by a vacancy.

This guide will help your organisation to hire effective people who are well-suited to the post, team and organisation. This may mean replacing staff when they leave, or it may entail hiring new staff for new positions. The information given is aimed primarily at hiring someone relatively junior, but most of it will also apply to senior hires. The section on search firms is particularly relevant to the latter.

If managed effectively, the whole recruitment process can be a marketing tool. It is an opportunity for the nonprofit organisation (NPO) to make a favourable impression on each and every candidate, who may in turn recount a positive experience to others. And of course one never knows who will become interested in the work of the NPO. Someone unsuccessful in his or her bid to become paid staff may decide to volunteer to help the organisation in other ways.

PLANNING FOR STAFF TURNOVER

Staff turnover is a fact of life. Making the right replacement decision is not just about the choice on interview day. It is about planning for vacancies, correctly assessing the needs of the job and the way it will fit into the team, and communicating the role and the organisation accurately to potential candidates and to other members of the job panel.

What provision is your team making for the reality that staff can and will leave? Do you have one member of staff solely responsible for a project or task, or for managing important contacts? Is anyone else aware of the work he or she is doing? Could a colleague take over if necessary? Are sufficient records being kept, so that a new member of staff could pick up the projects? Is it clear where she goes for help and advice, who her key contacts are, how her databases are managed? If only one person holds vital information, your organisation is at risk. At best her knowledge and expertise will be lost if she leaves; at worst, whole projects may have to be abandoned or started again from scratch.

Consider asking each member of staff to prepare a narrative of what he or she does including crucial information such as codes, passwords and PIN numbers for those pieces of equipment or contacts that require them, as well as important telephone numbers or e-mail addresses of contacts needed to do the job and other information vital to the smooth running of that particular post. Not only is this necessary in case staff members leave but it also is useful in case of illness or other absence.

When notified of an impending departure, it is tempting to quickly find an exact replacement of the person who is leaving. This is not necessarily the most appropriate course of action and may result in missing opportunities to improve the status quo.

Look at the existing job description if there is one. (If there is not, ask the post holder to draft one before he or she leaves.) Does it still provide a true reflection of the job the person is doing? The chances are that technology and processes will have changed, the job may have expanded to include responsibilities that are not mentioned, and there may be additional tasks that could be incorporated in the job.

Consult with others in the organisation before making decisions. Talk to superiors about the direction of the team. Perhaps some elements of the team's work are to be expanded, and others are to be phased out. How does this affect the skills required of the new post holder?

Talk to other team members about their interests, skills and ambitions to see if this is an opportunity to reassign a number of tasks. It is important that this early consultation process is treated as an information-gathering exercise and that promises are not made until a full picture is gathered. It may be that the vacancy does not need to be filled by a full-time staff member. It may be cheaper to outsource work to agencies or freelancers, or to offer a part-time post or short-term contract.

If you are filling a new role or the organisation is too small to have teams or others to consult with, filling a vacancy is still an opportunity to think through the position to be filled and whether it has changed or could be changed. Looking at similar organisations may also help you make decisions about the job to be filled.

Recruiting staff takes time. This is unavoidable. It is possible to organise temporary cover at a day's notice or even less, but to fill a permanent vacancy effectively can take months. By planning a timeline, you can estimate when you may realistically have someone in the post. Provision for the interim period can then be made, leaving the manager free to recruit the best person for the permanent job.

The following outlines the usual recruitment process:

1. PREPARING WRITTEN MATERIALS
It is likely that the job description, person specification, and information about the organisation will need to be rewritten, updated or drafted from scratch. It may be necessary to design or draft an advertisement or prepare a brief for an agency. Such materials may need to be signed off on by senior management.

2. ADVERTISING
Generally advertising space needs to be booked at least days and sometimes weeks in advance. If you have asked an agency to find appropriate candidates, the agency will need at least a few days to forward appropriate curricula vitae (CV) or resumes.

Reviewer's Comment
What is the difference between a CV and a resume? In some countries, there is almost no difference and the words are used interchangeably to mean information about a candidate's work and educational background. In other places, there is a considerable difference.

3. APPLICATIONS
Candidates should be given between two and three weeks to respond to advertisements requiring them to complete and return application forms by post. If it is simply a case of e-mailing a CV, this can be shortened.

4. SHORTLISTS
After the closing date for applications, a couple of days or more may be needed to make a shortlist of the best candidates. All those on the selection panel should be involved and will need to block time out of their schedules to devote to this. If a high level of response is expected, it may take much longer.

Continues on next page

5. INTERVIEWS

A date or dates for interviews should be scheduled with all members of the selection panel from an early stage. Candidates, once invited for an interview, should be given a week to prepare.

6. SECOND INTERVIEWS

If a second interview is required, allow candidates up to another week to prepare, particularly if there is a presentation or other test.

7. DECISIONS

A decision usually will be made within a day or two of seeing all the candidates, providing all decision makers will be available at this time. The successful candidate can then be notified immediately.

8. REFERENCES

It may take a week or more to get permission to contact referees, to make contact, and to get the information needed from them.

9. NOTICE PERIODS

The new post holder is likely to have to give at least a month's notice to his or her current employer and much longer for senior positions.

So it is important to realistically assess the time it will take to fill a vacancy. It will almost certainly mean getting a temp or volunteer as a stop-gap measure, or asking another member of the staff to step into the vacant role, or formally redistributing essential tasks of the post being vacated.

ADVERTISING INTERNALLY

Some organisations have a policy on internal recruitment and promotion. Find out what this is as there may be a requirement that all vacancies are offered internally first. If not, consider the advantages and disadvantages of offering the post internally. It helps retain knowledge and expertise in the organisation, and internal candidates will already know their colleagues and the organisation's ethics, values and processes, which should enable them to settle into the role quickly. It may help to assure continuity of projects and relationships. In general it can have a positive effect on staff morale and performance to know that promotion is a realistic possibility. Conversely, bringing in someone from outside the organisation brings new ideas and the expertise of other organisations that may have different strengths from your own. This can add immense value. It may also change the dynamics among colleagues, many times for the good.

You may choose to advertise both internally and externally simultaneously. This gives the best chance of finding the best candidate because you can compare all potential applicants. But it does run the risk of alienating existing staff, especially if someone internally believes he or she is well-qualified for the role. It also wastes funds to advertise externally if a good candidate is already available within the organisation.

It may be preferable to promote a vacancy internally first, and then to look outside if it is not filled. The difficulty here is that you are trying to compare an internal candidate with an unknown external field of candidates.

This decision must be taken by each NPO, depending on the size of the organisation, the nature of the post, the needs of the team, the values and culture of the organisation, and the resources available.

AGENCIES

Many agencies specialise in the NPO sector. Agencies are useful for getting a selection of CVs quickly, enabling comparison of many candidates, and they are useful if a job requires specialist skills or experience. Generally they only charge for their services if you appoint one of their candidates. They take a lot of time-consuming paperwork away from the NPO by only passing on CVs that are

Continues on next page

appropriate. On the other hand, their role in attracting CVs is relatively passive; they are dependent on the unemployed and those actively job-hunting who register with them. Furthermore, it is necessary to ensure that there is some value added in their service (e.g., that the candidates whose CVs they submit have been interviewed or screened in some way); otherwise, they are merely acting as a clearinghouse.

Always check agency fees before you accept CVs, and try to negotiate a preferential rate, especially if the organisation has a lot of vacancies that an agency may be asked to fill.

MASS-MARKET PUBLICATIONS

It may be appropriate to advertise the position in newspapers and other publications. You need to determine which ones are most appropriate for the job being advertised and for the sector in which your organisation works. National newspapers or magazines or those with large circulations will generally attract a larger response. Such advertisements are generally costly, but it may be possible for an NPO to negotiate a

lower price, a larger advertisement for the same cost, an extra insertion for free or advertisements in related publications at no additional cost. Ensure that your advertisement appears on the publication's Web site.

Rates are generally lower in small or local publications, and the likelihood of preferential rates, free insertions or related advertising is higher, especially if you can build up a relationship with the publication.

Some mass-market newspapers cater more to the NPO sector or are known for their NPO advertisements. It is worth finding out if this is true in your area.

SPECIALIST PUBLICATIONS

Many newspapers and journals have an NPO advertisement section. Their advertising rate may be cheaper, and they have the advantage of being targeted at exactly the right audience. However, their circulation is often much lower than mass-market publications, and the narrow audience might preclude responses from those who may be right for the job but have not worked in the NPO sector or do not read that particular publication.

ADVERTISING A VACANCY

Depending on the job to be filled, a combination of advertisements both within the sector and within the general community may be desirable.

INTERNET
It costs nothing to post a vacancy on your NPO's own Web site; however, this is unlikely to be seen by most external job seekers, unless they are specifically committed to working for your organisation.

There are a number of job Web sites that are likely to attract applicants for your particular vacancy — there are many sites devoted to specialist jobs or specialist fields.

THE ADVERTISEMENT
The advertisement you place should stimulate interest and draw people to apply, while at the same time giving a realistic impression of the job. Misleading potential applicants simply wastes your time and theirs. Follow legal

requirements, if any, and avoid jargon that may not be widely understood.

The advertisement should include:

- Job title
- Organisation's name
- Salary details
- Location of job
- Brief description of organisation's purpose
- Brief outline of responsibilities/ nature of job
- Brief criteria for eligibility – skills/qualifications/experience
- Whom to contact for information, how to contact them and how to apply
- Closing date for applications
- Declaration of charitable status or other required information about your organisation

Continues on next page

Reviewer's Comment

This guide is focused primarily on how to manage the recruitment process in-house. For more senior appointments or where there is a need for discretion (e.g., the present incumbent is unaware he or she is to be replaced/sidelined) or confidentiality (staff can be demoralised to learn of the impending departure of a popular, effective CEO), it is worth considering the possibility of outsourcing the process to a search firm.

Broadly speaking, executive search can be divided into (1) advertising and selection and (2) search. Some firms do both. As its name implies, the former involves placing advertisements in the (inter)national press, selecting and interviewing candidates, then presenting a shortlist to the client. In addition to passing on the cost of the advertisements (which can be significant), firms charge about 17 percent of the first year's compensation.

One of the main drawbacks of the advertising and selection option is that the best candidates may not be scanning the Situations Vacant columns. In the search option, a firm targets qualified individuals who are not necessarily looking for a new challenge or who may not currently be working in the same sector but have the right skill sets, etc. Search can be further divided into contingency and retained search. In the former, there is no upfront payment, and a fee of 20 percent to 25 percent of the first year's compensation is only charged if a candidate is placed. The main focus of contingency search firms is using their existing databases, and relatively little real search is done because it is too expensive and too high-risk. Retained search is the most expensive option but it guarantees results. Thirty percent to 33 percent of the first year's compensation is commonly paid in three instalments, the first third being paid on signing the contract with the NPO. The firm uses every possible means of tracking down potential candidates – customised research, databases, networking, etc. – until the right person is found.

You may want to have an application pack to send to applicants for the job. The aim of the pack is to give potential candidates all of the information they will need to decide whether to apply, and then to make their application. Remember, you will need to compare all candidates equally, so they should all receive the same information and be given the same instruction, regardless of how they heard about the job. The pack should give a realistic impression of the job to be filled in order to attract people whose interests, skills and ambitions match its requirements. In order to test the candidates against the criteria for the job, the pack should also elicit appropriate and relevant information for those interviewing the candidates and making the decision about whom to hire.

Once an advertisement appears, the response will be immediate. Ensure that a number of application packs are made up in advance to cope with this.

An application pack is likely to include:

- Letter from the organisation
- Job description
- Person specification
- Background information about the team and the organisation
- Application form (unless CVs only are invited)

THE LETTER

The letter should give details of what candidates need to do to apply, what to expect once they have applied, and whom to contact should they need further information. The closing date for application must be clear. It is helpful to list all items enclosed in the pack so recipients can ensure they have received all materials.

If you do not intend to respond to unsuccessful applicants, this should be explained. Otherwise, you will waste time fielding telephone calls from interested but unsuccessful applicants. With senior appointments, it is a good practice to acknowledge all applications and to send a standard but nicely worded rejection letter to unsuccessful candidates.

THE JOB DESCRIPTION

The job description should include:

- Job title
- Salary range

Continues on next page

- Where the job is based
- Whether the contract is full time, part time, permanent, fixed term
- Who the post holder reports to and who reports to the post holder
- Brief summary of the purpose of the post
- Main responsibilities and accountabilities

When drafting the job description, refer to broader plans to ensure that the job is positioned within the organisational and team objectives.

THE PERSON SPECIFICATION

This document sets out the criteria for the successful candidate. It should include specific requirements in terms of:

- Qualifications (e.g., degree(s), professional qualifications)
- Experience (what they have done, previous jobs)
- Knowledge (what they know or understand, e.g., language and IT skills)
- Skills (abilities such as decision making, communication, organisation)

It may be helpful to divide these into criteria that are essential and those that are desirable. This helps candidates to decide whether they are eligible and also aids the shortlist process.

ORGANISATIONAL INFORMATION

This gives the candidates some background on the organisation they are thinking of joining. It would be helpful to include:

- The nature of the organisation – what does it exist to do?
- How it achieves its mission
- The size of the organisation – number of staff, annual income
- The values and ethics and aims of the organisation
- How the candidate's prospective job or team fits into the organisation
- The main challenges that will affect the role advertised
- Pay scheme, pensions, any other benefits and schemes that may affect the post holder
- Where the candidate can go for further information about the organisation (e.g., the organisation's Web site)

Remember, the organisation needs to attract the right candidate to the role as much as the candidate needs to appeal to the selectors (and match him or herself to the organisation). The post should be presented in a positive and appealing, but realistic, light.

APPLICATION FORM/CV

If you use an application form, this could be the only information you obtain from each candidate to make your initial selections. Include everything you will need to know to make a decision and to contact them. For example: name, address, telephone number, E-mail address, education, any professional qualifications or courses, work experience, references, previous convictions or other information that may preclude an applicant from being employed, and a supporting statement from the applicant about his or her interest in and suitability for the job.

It is important to plan the whole application process from the start so that candidates receive the right information about what is expected from them. For example, will a CV be considered as well as, or instead of, an application form? Will there be a test as well as an interview? Will there be a second interview?

Referring to the person specification, decide which criteria must be met and which tools to use to test these criteria. For example:

- Application form
- CV
- Interview
- Presentation
- Psychometric testing
- Numeric or verbal reasoning tests
- Personality tests
- Unseen situational test

Many tests are available from books, Web sites, HR departments, and agencies. Some need to be assessed by professionals or experts to be effective; this may or may not be a worthwhile investment. Other tests more specific to the vacancy are better devised in-house. Seek advice from colleagues, HR departments, or contacts in other organisations to get started. Think about typical or challenging situations that the employee may find him/herself in e.g., prioritising contents of an in-tray, drafting a difficult letter, completing accurate entries on a database, calculating budgets, or presenting a new proposal.

THE SELECTION PANEL

It is usual to have two or three people on an interview panel, perhaps more if the vacancy is particularly technical or senior. The potential employee's line manager should certainly be one of them. The panel should include:

- At least one experienced or trained interviewer

- Someone with a close understanding of any specialist skills required

- Someone trained in equal opportunity/discrimination legislation

All should be at least as senior as the post being appointed, providing the above requirements can be met.

Reviewer's Comment

In many places, it won't be necessary to have someone specially trained in equal opportunity/discrimination. Many of these issues will be commonly known.

Ensure that the panel members are well briefed. Who will be involved in devising shortlists? Is everyone in agreement about what you are looking for in the successful candidate? Will one person have the final decision if you cannot agree?

In the interview itself, who will take the lead (i.e., who will welcome the candidate, introduce the panel, explain the format of the interview, and introduce the organisation and vacancy)? Who will ask which questions? Who will be first to follow up if an answer requires more depth? Who will take notes? Who will take the candidate's questions? Who will close the interview and show the candidate out?

For those organisations too small to have a panel made up of employees, it may be appropriate to ask trustees or legal or accounting advisors to participate in the selection process. Even if the decision is to be made by one person, much of the process that follows will be applicable.

Applications should be viewed against the criteria of the person specification to establish objectively who should be placed on a shortlist to be interviewed. In the interest of fairness, previous knowledge of candidates should not be taken into account at this stage, and candidates should all get the same instructions, so that the information they supply is comparable.

The panel should be in agreement about the most important functions of the job, as well as the most important qualifications, skills, knowledge, and experience. The panel grades applications against each requirement of the person specification, perhaps by giving a mark out of 10.

It is helpful for each member of the panel to make a provisional shortlist independently, then for all to meet to agree on a final list. If each list is very different, now is the time to check each panel member's understanding of the criteria. Clarifying this will avoid confusion later. It is unusual to interview more than six people, unless the vacancy is particularly important or the field is particularly strong. It is clearly not necessary to interview six if the field is poor. There is no point interviewing a weak applicant to make up numbers.

Reviewer's Comment

The number of candidates you short-list will depend on the type of position being filled as well as the strength of the field. Search firms will regularly short-list as many as they feel appropriate for the position.

To short-list quickly, block out time in the panel members' schedules in advance so that they can give their attention to applications within a day or two of the closing date. Remember, applicants may be applying for other jobs as well; a good candidate may be offered another post while waiting to hear from you.

A written record should be kept showing the reasoning behind all shortlist decisions. It helps to eliminate subjectivity from the process, keeps decisions transparent, and helps if applicants request feedback.

Interviews can be arranged by letter, by phone, or even by E-mail. Remember, it may not be easy for the person to talk freely; always check first whether a call would be convenient or an E-mail would be appropriate. It may be difficult for the candidate to attend an interview during working hours, especially at short notice or if it involves travelling. It may be necessary to interview over a number of days. Find out when the panel members are available, so that you can offer alternatives if the candidate cannot meet at a suggested time.

The interview gives you an opportunity to meet the candidate; to verify and expand on the information given in a written application; and to test the skills, knowledge and experience that are needed for the role. It also gives the candidate an opportunity to find out more about the vacancy and the organisation, and to assess whether it is the right job for him or her.

INTERVIEW PRACTICALITIES

Interview rooms may need to be booked days or weeks in advance. In order to protect the confidentiality of candidates, interviews may need to be conducted off-site. Is the room suitable? Will an overhead projector or other presentation equipment be needed? Will a second room be required for tests?

Will someone other than the interviewer be welcoming the candidates and showing them to the appropriate rooms? Everyone affected by the interview process should be briefed appropriately. For example, the receptionist should be aware of candidates' arrival times. If candidates are to be shown around their prospective work area, then other staff affected should be notified in advance.

The scene that is set should be appropriate to the style of interview. Sitting next to the candidate suggests informality, a panel lined up in a row opposite the candidate appears confrontational, and two people facing each other across an empty desk is formal. There should be no distractions in the area (such as telephones or computer screens), and provision should be made to avoid interruptions.

Continues on next page

Reviewer's Comment
The cultural issues implied in the style of interview will vary from place to place. Talk to others about their experiences and feelings regarding interview styles if you are uncertain what would be appropriate for your organisation or for this particular recruitment.

Interview times should be scheduled far enough apart to provide adequate time for the interview plus time between candidates for the interviewers to make notes, to discuss the last interview, and to clear their minds before the next meeting. It creates a bad impression to keep candidates waiting, and rushing from one interview to the next can make candidates blur in panel members' minds.

CONDUCTING THE INTERVIEW
Remember that you are an ambassador for your organisation and act accordingly. You may need to promote the vacancy as vigorously as the candidate is promoting him or herself.

Reviewer's Comment
Be careful not to oversell the position or paint too rosy a picture of the organisation. Candidates hired under false pretences tend to underperform or leave the organisation.

Interviews can be held in different ways, depending on the skills being tested. For example, it may be friendly and informal to encourage relaxed information sharing, or it may be confrontational and aggressive to see how someone performs under pressure.

Questions may explore someone's background, asking for factual information about experience gained (e.g., "What were the main functions of your last job?"). Or questions may place someone in a hypothetical situation, to test how he or she might react (e.g., "You are on the phone to an irate supporter who has received three letters since requesting not to receive any literature. What do you say?"). Or they may be technical questions, to explore someone's understanding of a particular task or system (e.g., "How would you store x information on a database?").

Open questions are designed to elicit lots of information; they give the interviewee a chance to share views and experience (e.g., "Tell me about a time you had to make a difficult decision at work. What happened?"). They should not be structured to lead to a particular answer.

Closed questions lead to a yes/no answer and are useful for verifying information (e.g., "So you took a six-month break between leaving your first job and starting your second?").

Use active listening skills – the interviewer(s) should be talking approximately 20 percent of the time, and the interviewee 80 percent. If you are unclear about what a candidate is saying, ask for clarification.

You should have a set of core questions that all candidates will answer, so that the information obtained is comparable for all candidates. This does not mean that you cannot deviate from the script to push a point or to get clarity where needed. Ensure that the questions give you the opportunity to assess candidates' suitability against all criteria.

Candidates should always be given the opportunity to ask questions of their prospective employer. Ensure that you have prepared answers to likely questions.

Even if you have quickly decided that a candidate is unsuitable for the job, complete the full interview and end it politely, without rushing to a conclusion. This person may not be right for this post, but your paths may cross again in the future.

A written record should be kept from each interview. This ensures the objectivity of the process and facilitates giving feedback. It is also useful for the successful interviewee; it may remind you of strengths, weaknesses and training needs to explore once he or she starts work.

THE SELECTION DECISION

Each candidate should be evaluated against the person specification as the interview progresses. Some organisations simply give a mark out of 10 for each criterion and offer the job to the person with the highest score. Others allow more subjectivity, giving consideration to how the individual might fit into the existing team and organisation.

Take time to consider all candidates. It can help to reflect silently alone at first, then to discuss the candidates' relative merits with the other members of the panel to clarify impressions and reach agreement.

If the panel cannot agree, you may:
- Allow one member of the panel to make the final decision.

- Recall two or more candidates for additional discussion.

- Re-advertise for more candidates. Consider using different means of promotion or changing the advertisement to attract different people.

NOTIFICATION OF CANDIDATES

Contact the first-choice candidate as soon as possible to establish whether he or she will accept the post, if references are acceptable. Be aware that you may be contacting the candidate at work so be discreet in introducing yourself. Discuss the candidate's notice period or other obligations at his/her current job and agree to a provisional start date. Explain the salary offer and provide a contact number should he/she think of any more questions.

If someone has accepted, you can then contact the unsuccessful applicants, either by letter, phone or personal e-mail. Give verbal or written feedback if required. Providing constructive feedback helps to create a positive impression of you and your organisation.

EVALUATION/LEGAL ISSUES

EVALUATING THE RECRUITMENT PROCESS

Once an appointment is made, evaluate the process. Note what worked well and what did not so that future recruitments can be quicker, cheaper, or better planned and executed. For example, where did the best applicants come from? Did most people who requested a pack apply, or did something put them off? Was the recruitment cost-effective? Were the chosen tests or questions effective in eliciting helpful information? Was the panel well-chosen – did everyone contribute different perspectives or experiences?

Document the findings from the evaluation. Keep a record of the contact details of agencies and firms used and publications where advertisements appeared. Keep unsuccessful applicants on file (providing you have told them you will do so) in case of future vacancies or requests for feedback.

LEGAL ISSUES AND BEST PRACTICE

It is the responsibility of each recruiter to be aware of the laws governing recruitment in his or her own country. Legal requirements, best practice, and penalties for abuse vary from country to country. Some issues that may be affected by legal requirements are:

- Where you advertise and what media and languages you use
- The way advertisements and interview questions are phrased
- What questions interviewers can ask
- Selection decisions
- The overall profile of the organisation's work force
- Necessity for employment contracts
- Requirements regarding the job itself

FINAL THOUGHTS

The people you recruit determine the success or failure of your organisation. It is not a case of what their contribution is to the organisation. They are the organisation.

The importance of the task cannot be overstated. It is worth taking the time and effort to prepare properly and to get it right.

CAROLINE HUKINS

Caroline Hukins has worked in the nonprofit sector in the UK for more than 10 years, both as a volunteer fundraiser and a professional.

Following university she won a place on the National Society for the Prevention of Cruelty to Children (NSPCC) graduate trainee program in Fundraising Appeals, and subsequently worked on the multimillion-pound Full Stop Campaign for the Millennium.

She spent 18 months organising overseas biking and trekking challenges for Macmillan Cancer Relief, generating over $1 million from this type of fundraising.

She then spent 3 years managing a wide-ranging events program at the National Asthma Campaign, including sporting events, overseas challenges, sponsored activities, ticketed special events and wider community fundraising.

Caroline now works as a freelance author and editor and leads charity treks and bike rides all over the world.

Judith Hare, Reviewer

A modern languages graduate, Judith started her career in the public sector doing economic research at the Bank of England. Her move to Belgium in the late 1970s brought with it a move into the private sector and general management. After successfully completing her MBA, she embarked on a couple of entrepreneurial ventures.

Judith moved into executive search 13 years ago, working initially for a contract research firm. Since 1996, she has been an Associate with Hansar International, a leading transnational search firm in Brussels.